The Ir.

Don't Turn Away

Words: David Hamilton
Illustration: Jacob Yerex

Saori

Words: Samantha Young
Illustration: Jacob Yerex

Witch

Jacob Yerex

A Creeping blindness

Words: David Hamilton
Illustration: Jacob Yerex

Morphogenesis

Jacob Yerex

The Loathing

Jacob Yerex

The Forming

Jacob Yerex

Grandmotherchild

Jacob Yerex

Portal

Jacob Yerex

One Printers Way
Altona, MB R0G0B0,
Canada

www.friesenpress.com

Copyright © 2022 by Jacob Yerex
First Edition — 2022

All rights reserved.

No part of this publication may be reproduced in any form, or by any means, electronic or mechanical, including photocopying, recording, or any information browsing, storage, or retrieval system, without permission in writing from FriesenPress.

ISBN
978-1-03-911938-3 (Hardcover)
978-1-03-911937-6 (Paperback)
978-1-03-911939-0 (eBook)

1. POETRY, SUBJECTS & THEMES, NATURE

Distributed to the trade by The Ingram Book Company

Don't Turn Away

Don't turn away.

Don't move. Be still.

Let time and place drift aimlessly.

Make here a place where there is no intention,

make the present a moment
that will never be.

I wish eternity to be the present moment.

I wish to remain in
this very place.

To be aimless is to
be content.

SAORI
(Three syllables Sa O Ri)

I am Saori

I came to her in a dream

A sweet lullaby

She asked me my name

I told her it's Saori

That's when I became

Her silk still shines bright

The years cannot be covered

By the weight of life

WITCH

WITCH!

I meant it as a compliment.
I am also a witch.

Intuition, serendipity, coincidence

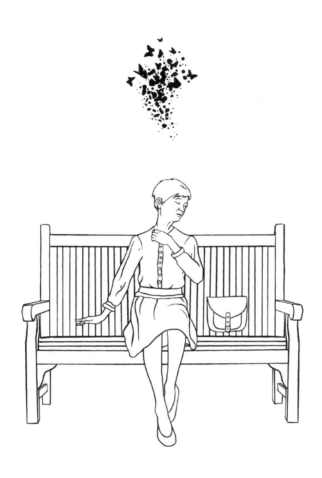

Faith, hope, inspiration . . . love.
These are magic.

Your intuition of others' intention.
Your clarity of mind.
Your clarity of heart.

Your ability to truly listen and understand what another feels.

These are all magic.

Now you are in your make-believe.

Relax and concentrate.
You can stay there.
Just look around.

Your thoughts affect reality.

There are dimensions where thoughts exist as objects like matter exists in this dimension.

A witch uses the make-believe
to affect this reality.
Everyone does this, but a witch
knows they are doing it.

A CREEPING BLINDNESS

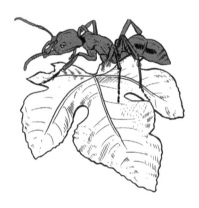

Moments of pleasure

passing as peace.

Seed the violent.

Annihilation.

A creeping blindess

fed by plenitude,

clouding the bleak futures

of those to come.

Waking glimpses of recognition

reveal the horrors.

Buried by greed.

MORPHOGENESIS

Sometimes, it starts as a sound.

I can feel it, hear it, and see it,
all at the same time.

Sometimes I believe it to be part of me.

It told me it was trying to take on a human form.

I thought it was all in my mind
until I touched it.

By touching me it can
mimic human genomes.

I am encouraged to explore.

The concentration required to sustain the form is fatiguing.

It asked me if I could teach it to fly.

I said that I didn't know how to fly.

We are making progress.

I find myself waiting
for the next encounter.

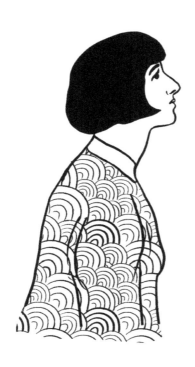

THE LOATHING

It starts at the back of my neck,
like a bird landing on a nest.

A shadow, dark and brooding.

It makes my heart quicken
and my breath short.

It shadows me,
painting bleak futures.

It is loathing, self-loathing.

Sometimes I believe it to
be part of me.

I decided to look at it,
really look at it.

It turned in on itself, it was sticky.

It became smaller, and I could recognize myself separate from it..

It evaporated.

THE FORMING

It's different than the other ones.

The other ones are shadows.

This has form or is forming.

It's playful and responsive, and
I somehow feel connected to it.

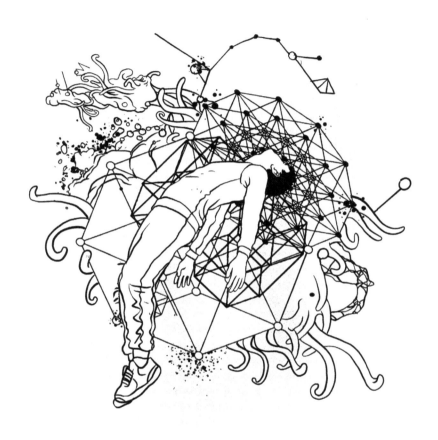

I can change it with my thoughts.
Sometimes I believe it to be part of me.

In the beginning it would
just show up in my daydreams.

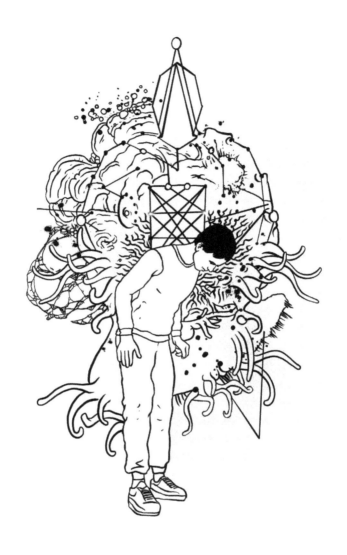

I converse with it in my head, but separating it from my own thoughts can be difficult.

I think it's trying to
teach me something.

It shows me shapes and geometry
that I feel, like emotions.

Sometimes I grasp it
for fleeting moments.

Then it disappears
like a fading dream.

GRANDMOTHERCHILD

I have been around the cycle so many times that I can't remember if I am being born or dying.

Sometimes I think that there is only flux.

An endless gradation between
being and not being.

Infinity negates the concept of time.

Dying is forgetting what
I thought I was.

Being born is forgetting what I am.

I am constant through the flux.

I am an hourglass in zero gravity.

I am many names, but I am not a name.

Grandmother call me Grandchild.

Grandchild call me Grandmother.

I am the middle that we slip through.

I see us on the other side.

PORTAL

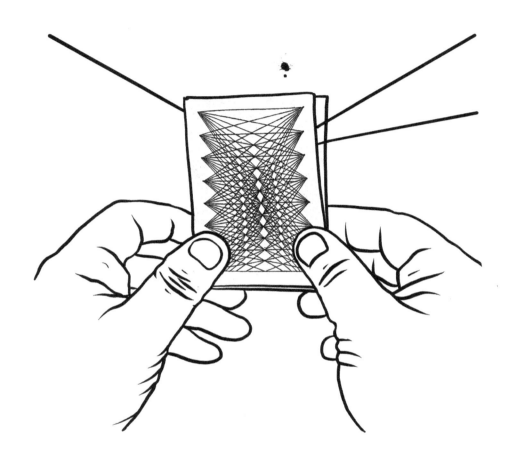

She suggested I create a doorway.

You can use a folded piece of paper.

Unfold the piece of paper when you want to enter the doorway.

Imagine a portal between the physical and psychic worlds.

Energy moves between the worlds when the door is open.

We carry information through the portal,
among other things.

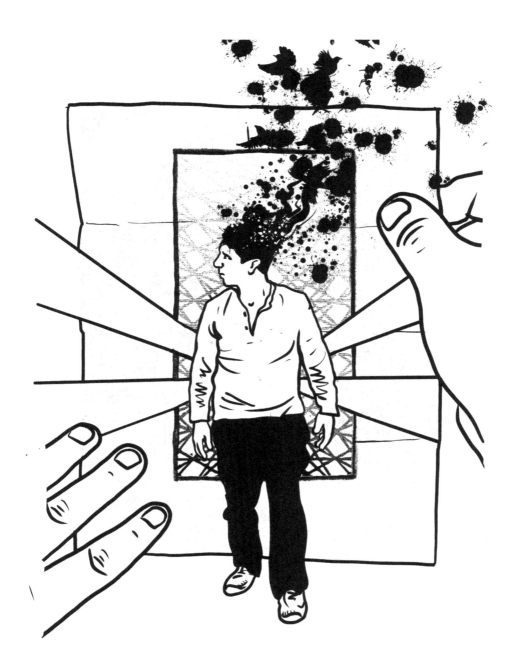

Make the use of the door a deliberate act.

She told me to fold the paper back up when I was done.

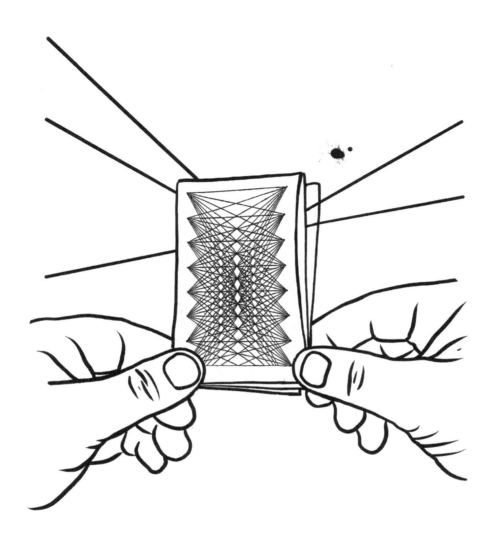

Don't forget to close the door.

CPSIA information can be obtained
at www.ICGtesting.com
Printed in the USA
BVHW091010211022
649931BV00004B/19